I0475103

This book is an executive summary of historic events that explain current economic and social changes and the necessary emergence of the cryptographic protocol and its first electronic medium of exchange; Bitcoin.

Published by: IBEX Press

Copyright © 2014 by R. Frank Tulak
First Edition, 2014

Published in the United States of America

ISBN: 978-1-312-20893-3

Table of Contents

CHAPTER	PAGE
What time is it?	1
Epoch	5
The Domesticated Horse	7
Steam Engine	11
The Airplane and Jet Age	15
The Original Purpose of Currency	19
The Era of Decentralization Begins	23
The First Financial Protocol	30
Exponential Growth	34
Rate of Accelerated Change	41
No Control	44
Unstoppable Train	47
Acknowledgements	49

Time Makes Money

***When we live inside a clock
it is difficult to know what time it is***

What time is it?

This question has been asked me by those without a watch or generally didn't care what time it was. The answer was always so many minutes after the present hour or so many minutes before the coming hour. For many people time is further divided into so many days till the weekend or vacation, or the coming day of graduation or promotion or their wedding day or the birth of their child. Then after that personal epoch moment they have entered a new personal era and time is measured from that moment on.

When I ask someone what era of historical time we as mankind are living in I find their answer depends on their education, personal experiences and personal or professional interests.

The most repeated answers have been: the Age of Aquarius; the Age of Technical Singularity; the Age of Trans humanism; the Sub Atlantic Age of the Holocene epoch; A.D.(C.E.); the Space Age; the Post Modernistic Age and the Computer Age.

These answers have puzzled me; because, if we know the path we are on as well as the velocity that we are traveling and the resources' required to power the travel and the motivation for the journey; then by examining all previous epochs and eras in comparison we should know where we are and when we will discover the next epoch and enter the next era.
With this understanding of an Age then we should know what do to maximize our efforts within the age we are in and be aware and recognize the next coming epoch.

The problem is our map is not the territory. In other words, if we are trying to use a map of the city we live in that is 150 years old we would quickly discover major discrepancies between the map and reality. Likewise if we left our city and did not return for 150 years we would find ourselves totally disorientated. This illustrates the problem of any projections of the future as well as perceptions of the past. Because everyone is comparing the past and future of mankind using the present personal scale of needs and values, as if these values have remained constant since the dawn of mankind. But when they are applied for the detection and projection of epochs and eras they prove to be of little to no value. The best research on the universal needs that motivate us and which transcend all eras of mankind is Maslow's hierarchy of needs.

These hierarchal needs begin with the basic motivators in life which are called **Physiological Needs** they are the needs that take priority over all other needs and are our dominate motivators. A few of our **Physiological Needs** that make up our prime motivation are the need for air, water, food and sex.

When an individual's physical needs are relatively satisfied, then the individual's **Safety and Security** needs take precedence and dominate our behavior; these needs that motivate us are security and protection of our body, our financial income, our family and our property.

When our individual **Safety and Security** needs are relatively met then and only then do we progress to the next level of needs that motivate us, the need to **Love and to Belong** which is the development of friendship, intimacy and family.

When the human need and motivation to feel a sense of **Love and Belonging,** an acceptance of another or among others, our membership in a social group then begins. We enter the next level of need and motivation which is **Esteem,** doing that which builds our self-confidence. We begin acquiring achievements, gaining the respect of others and begin to respect others as well.

These levels of needs that motivate us are built one upon another; if any components of the lower level of needs motivation become lost or missing then all the higher levels become meaningless and no longer have value to us until that need is fulfilled.

This explains why many great professionals, from astronauts to actors, to congressmen have destroyed their professions, ruined their friendships and family to fulfill a need at the physical level, it is just the way we are made.

As we look over mankind since his appearance as hunter-gather we see that survival was his primary concern. His time was spent hunting, gathering, preparing, and consuming. The more time spent hunting and gathering the greater amount of food he had; therefore **time makes food**.

With the epoch of farming, man had for the first time a surplus of food. This **Agricultural Era** began the necessity of the next level of need and motivation

Safety and Security. The protecting of surplus as well as family and possessions resulted in the growth and development of cities.

Now, with the basic food in surplus, the development of livestock and alternate crops as well as multiple township skills emerged. This emergence required a common unit of account in the market thus the creation of gold and silver money began to grow and dominate. Therefore the more time an individual gave to increasing his skill or in breeding of his livestock or crops the more silver and gold he received to buy food as well as other things he needed and wanted. This classic conditioning of relating food to money resulted in the unconscious perception that **time makes money**.

From this epoch point money becomes associated with the primary **Physiological Need** and greatest motivator; food.

Epoch

"On résiste à l'invasion des armées;
on ne résiste pas à l'invasion des idées."

More powerful than the might
of all the armies on Earth
is an idea whose time has come.
(Paraphr. Trans.)
Victor Hugo, Histoire d'un Crime (History of a Crime)
(written 1852, published 1877)

With water, the temperature of 212 degrees Fahrenheit is magical. The liquid substance metamorphoses into steam whose volume is 1600 times the volume it had in its previous state as a liquid. If the container is not designed for that expansion the container will be destroyed. This expansion does not happen to all the water molecules at once but as each molecule reaches that critical point of 212 degrees it expands to 1600 times its volume. This instant gargantuan expansion increases the pressure and temperature upon the other molecules forcing an acceleration of their conversion.

A slow motion video of a boiler explosion is very instructive and gives insight to every epoch in the history of man.

Watching the video you would witness the walls of the boiler begin to buckle under the stress of the pressure. Patches of the steel blister and bulge as if a ravenous monster was attempting to pound through the metal to escape. Seams would begin to detach, then a very small crack appears and then edges of the crack would peal back as the first jets of steam burst through to escape. Then all the steam attempts to exit that crack ripping and tearing the crack open, resulting in a massive explosion.

Why doesn't a kettle explode? Because as the expansion occurs it is allowed to exit the kettle through the spout until it is empty or the temperature drops back down below 212 degrees.

If the pressure has just begun, and there is a crack it functions as the spout of the kettle, allowing the expansion to escape. If the pressure continues to grow the escaping jet of steam will just widen the crack. If the expansion is forcibly contained and not allowed to escape the ultimate result will be the total destruction of that which contains it.

Eras don't encompass the whole of mankind at once but begin like the water turning to steam. The first molecule that turns to steam is the epoch signaling the coming era which then spreads to others though there is roaring steam there is still water in the container as well.

Are there still tribal nomadic hunter-gatherers? Are there cities of people who still using horse and buggy and do not use electricity? Why? Because those groups never reached that critical point even though the majority of others did.

Have we had an epoch? Yes, and the era has emerged with the internet (TCP/IP) and the decentralization of everything it touches.

Domesticated Horse

Since before the time of Alexander the Great and up to the First World War, commerce and communications were done at the speed of the horse. A horse could for a limited time do a full gallop and attain 25 to 30 mph, but at a walk was only 4 mph; not much faster than the speed of a walking man. But the horse at 4 mph could continue walking all day and carry supplies or when hitched to a wagon or stage coach could pull much more than any man could carry.

Combining the horse and wagon with the building of roads allowed the great Roman Empire to rise and dominate by transporting large quantities of goods, supplies and men great distances in less time.

The design of payments of gold and silver for goods and services were usually local transactions, no more than a few days journey and were done literally from the buyers hand to the hand of the seller, "hand over fist".

As the problem of distance increased it required a third or more parties to help cover the additional risks and costs of transactions done in silver or gold. Transactions over great distances required a national currency and the assistance of an organization whose representative could mediate the transaction at the distant location.

Business transactions at great distances could take months to years depending on the distance. Payments were sent or received in gold and silver bars, ingots or coins by well-guarded horse drawn coaches. This commercial limitation of delayed transactions caused a myriad amount of problems and complications. For instance payments could be stolen. Many times the purchaser died or the buying company collapsed before the transaction was complete. Imagine getting a communication, a simple letter or signed contract or authorization 2 to 3 months after its writing or signing.

This delay between the payment and the receipt to many was very valuable and termed "payment float" which allowed banks and large institutions to "play the float" giving the appearance of an asset that was in float to be used as collateral multiple times in transactions beyond what they actually held.

For Governments who issued the currency the float was not an option but deposits were required to be present before necessary withdraws. When the capital was insufficient the issuing government would debase the currency's silver or gold with an alloy stretching the amount of currency produced.

An excellent example of the debasement of currency was the Roman denarius.

Roman denarius
The denarius began as a 4.5 gram silver coin and had stayed that way for centuries under the Roman Republic. After Rome became an empire, things began to turn sour for the denarius and, by extension, the Roman economy. Base metals, such as copper were blended in with the silver and so even though the coin itself weighed the same, the amount of silver in it became less and less with each successive emperor. Throughout the first century the denarius contained over 90% silver but by the end of the second century the silver content had fallen to less than 70%.

A century later there was less than 5% silver in the coin and by 350 AD it was all but worthless, having an exchange rate of 4,600,000 to a gold solidus (or nearly 9 million to the original gold aureus).

A Roman citizen's daily wage, one silver denarius

Silver content of a Roman denarius

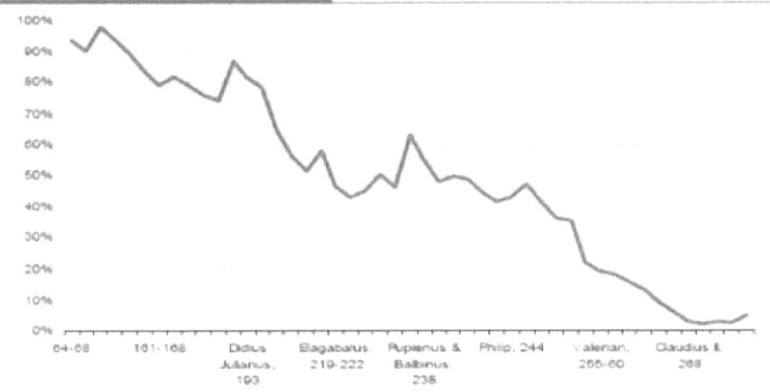

Source: http://www.tulane.edu/~august/handouts/601cpnn.htm

The economic chaos that the hyperinflation of the denarius had on Roman society was very real. The population of Rome reached a peak of about 1 million inhabitants during the first century BC and maintained that level until nearly the end of the second century. At this point it began to slowly decline throughout the third century and precipitously throughout the fourth. By the fifth century, only about 50 thousand people remained.

Bank Notes and Certificates of Deposit

Receipts of deposited gold, gold smiths receipts or later bank notes were not accepted and in many cases were illegal outside the city, state or territory in which they were issued. The great exception to this historically was during the Crusades with the depository of the Knights Templar where gold and silver were deposited in accounts with the Knights Templar in Rome and the receipt was redeemable in gold and silver at their castles in Jerusalem.

During the Pre-Civil War Era of the United States there were over 8000 different bank notes and their issuance greater than the amount of gold held. The rapid devaluing bank note was viewed as contemptible in many states. What amplified the devaluation of the bank note was the delay of redemption and those notes devaluation over that delay time making the bank note more like gambling than a store of value. The bank note was not wanted nor accepted and declared illegal in many outlying states and territories, preferring the acceptance of buck deer skins as a medium of exchange equaling $1 or a "buck".

This all changed after the completion of the intercontinental railroad and the wide acceptance of bank notes, especially US Government notes with the Treasury Note Act of July 14, 1890.

Steam Engine

The first great technological earthquake to shake the economic world, collapsing banks and bankrupting companies, was the utilization of the steam locomotive and completion of the transcontinental railroad.

This great invention killed the float time, traveling at five times the average speed of a horse. The steam locomotive could maintain the speed of a horse at full gallop, a velocity of 20 to 35 mph across the North American continent.

This disruptive technology changed every life in the country. Before its introduction, every town and city held their own perception of time, then all were forced to measure time the same way. The train would show up on its scheduled time and leave on its scheduled time. Those who were not there on time missed the train; if goods were not there on time they missed the train. At first ledgers which only had to make entries once a week were now required to make entries daily. Goods showed up in 1/5 the time demanding payment. Transactions were completed in weeks and months and no longer in months and years.

The railroad industry owned time and dictated the time in each city and controlled the movement of money.

These simultaneous transitions occurring weekly made the transport of bars, ingots or coins of silver and gold physically and financially impossible to mint and transport in time for each transaction, so the dreaded bank note became the standard medium of exchange with the Treasury Note Act of July 14, 1890.

To accelerate communication across the continent the invention of the Railroad Morse Code brought near instant communications to both sides of the country. Arrival times were set; goods delivery times were set and payment times were set; there was no float time. This decrease in transactional time made the bank note king.

As our nation approached 1901 the iron rails were replaced with steel rails increasing the steam locomotive's speed in excess of 70 miles per hour!

Then with the growth of the automobile and the building of roads and highways transactions occurred at higher frequencies thus the demand for paper currency exploded.

In the 1950s with the nationwide interstate freeways built, the automobile began to rival the train as the preferred method of travel between cities multiplying the demand for currency.

As the demand for bank notes exceeded the gold reserves that allowed their issuance, The Treasury despite this short fall would still authorize their printing and issuance to meet the demand.

With each presidential administration issuing more bank notes than gold reserves we see again the debasement of currency that occurred in Rome replayed again at the beginning of the last century.

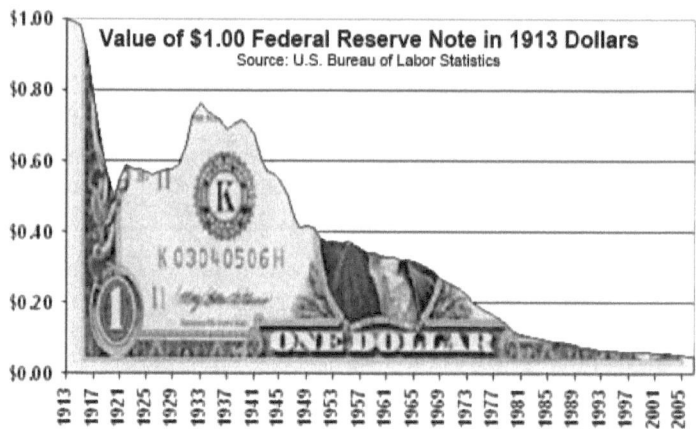

The Airplane and Jet Age

Though not as powerful an economic earthquake as the locomotive, the leap from the propeller airplane into the jet aircraft heralded the emergence of the jet age in the 1950's and commenced with the first commercial regularly scheduled transatlantic and transcontinental flights. With speeds in excess of 570 mph, passengers and goods would arrive across the Atlantic in a little over four hours. To say this caused an accounting nightmare is an understatement. How could a man make a purchase before he withdrew the money from the bank?
The problem of withdraws and expenditures of cash becoming temporally reversed was caused by the crossing of the time zones. Personal checks would not clear or the funds remained available even though they had been spent because the transaction happened according to the date/time stamp of the transaction, in the future.

Travelers had to bring all the money they would need to spend with them on the plane unless through foresight enough time was given to set up a bank account at the destination and transfer money to it before the traveler boarded his flight. For constant travelers to Europe the Swiss Bank Account was a necessity.

The solution was a third party mitigation which brought into existence a new medium of exchange to replace currency, the credit card, which would hold all the transactions and process them over a three week period. The first of these was the Diners Club card.

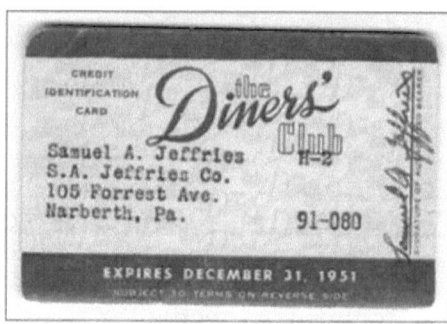

While overseas travel expenditures were being centralized though this new medium of financial exchange the "credit card"; the communications industry was experiencing explosive and crippling costs attempting to maintain the centralization of telephone communications nationwide.

Closest to physically being at a distant location was the ability to speak directly to an individual at great distances to express your own words and communicate directly to another, as it was said the telephone was "the next best thing to being there."
Since the inception of the telephone each call had to go through a third party; the switch board operator. As the acceptance of the telephone became an essential part of everyday life for all Americans so to the army of switch board operators swelled and correspondingly the costs of maintaining the expanding workforce escalated. The technology nearly collapsed under the weight of the cost to have an operator manage each call. The cost of centralization escalated and total collapse was inevitable.

THE HISTORY OF ESS (electronic switching system) (from "Telephone: The First Hundred Years" copyright 1975 & 1976 by Mr. Brooks, pages 278-279)

... As time dragged on and costs mounted, there was a concern at AT&T and something approaching panic at Bell Labs. But the project had to go forward; by this time the investment was too great to be sacrificed, and in any case, forward projections of increased demand for telephone service indicated that within a few years a time would come when, without the quantum leap in speed and flexibility that electronic switching would provide, the national network would be unable to meet the demand.... Kappel's tone on the subject in the 1964 annual report was, for him, an almost apologetic: "Electronic switching equipment must be manufactured in volume to unprecedented standards of reliability.... To turn out the equipment economically and with good speed, mass production methods must be developed; but, at the same time, there can be no loss of precision..." Another year and millions of dollars later, on May 30, 1965, the first commercial [electronic] central office was put into service at Succasunna, New Jersey.

With the decentralization of the telephone, through the Electronic Switching System, the requirement of a third party (operator) to connect the caller with the receiver on the other end of the line was no longer needed but allowed each caller through dialing the area code first then the number gave near instant communication and cut the costs of operation nearly in half!

With more additional funds for research pulse dialing gave way to tone dialing, opening the door to the greatest economic earthquake of all; the internet.

The Original Purpose of Currency

Currency in its original purpose was to provide a common unit of account that was accepted by all participants. It was a one to one exchange dropping from the open hand of the buyer to the closing hand of the seller; hand over fist. The transaction was complete and immediate upon receipt of payment for goods or services.

The more distant the transactions the more time it took for the transaction to occur which greatly increased the cost and risk.

Therefore an additional member was necessary to add to the transaction; a merchant, financier or banker. By joining the transaction would facilitate the distant transaction reducing risk and possible loss in the transaction, for a fee.

Then, historically, the government or its agent eventually replaces the third member and becomes the sole intermediary and centralizes all transactions disallowing all others. After exclusivity has been established and the currency centralized, the currency begins to be debased. As the perceived demand for additional governmental centralization increases and with it the corresponding escalating costs to maintain centralization; the additional revenue is effortlessly acquired through currency debasement.

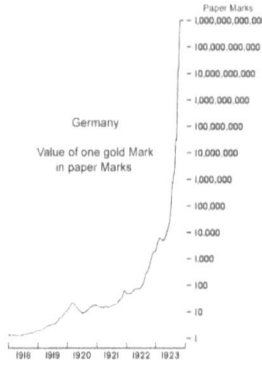

This debasement continues until the government nears collapse which in its desperation, increases tax revenue from its overburdened citizens or justifies war with another nation to take that other nation's resources. Because these actions only provide a temporary relief and because the cause of which is the high cost of over centralization, requiring further currency debasement to survive has not been arrested, the country finally collapses. This results in the rise of a new government and a new centralized currency and the cycle begins again.

At left a medal commemorating Germany's 1923 hyperinflation. The engraving reads:
"On 1st November 1923
1 pound of bread cost 3 billion,
1 pound of meat: 36 billion,
1 glass of beer: 4 billion."

Currency's primary purpose is a store of value; once it becomes debased or inflated it can no longer be accurately called "money".

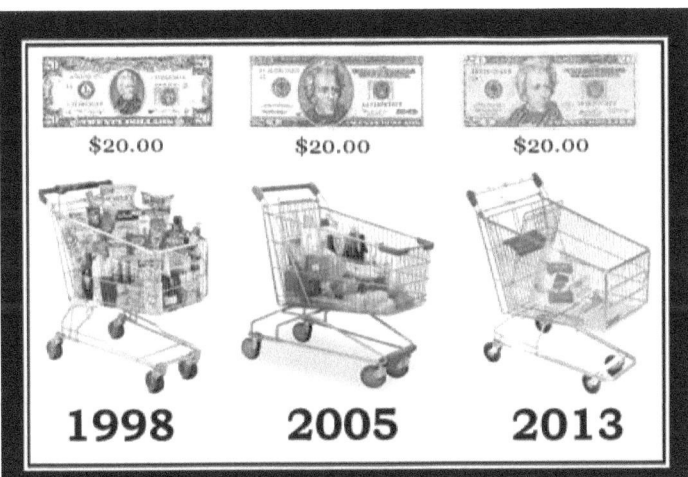

The original purpose of a currency is:

- A common unit of account between two individuals beyond boundaries or borders
- Rare or limited supply
- Maintains value
- Fungible
- Easily broken into equal fractional amounts
- Cannot be inflated or debased
- No third party mediator
- No additional costs
- Transaction time is equivalent to the time transpired in opening of ones purse and extracting the appropriate amount of currency then placing that amount into the hands of another.

The following demonstrates how gold still holds reign over all currencies that have ever existed.

1908
Ford Motor Company produced
The *Coupelet*

Cost **14 one once gold coins**
Fill the gas tank for...
1/40 an ounce of gold

2012
Toyota Motor Corporation
The *Camry*

Cost **14 one once gold coins**
Fill the gas tank for......
1/40 an ounce of gold

Era of Decentralization Begins

Starting with Bell Labs invention of the transistor and the electronic circuit switch which provided direct dialing without a third person the technology continued to develop. The next development was that of the IC chip. The chip provided multiple transistors for complex switching which changed the teletype; where one letter or number was sent from one location to another over a single circuit, to where pages of text could be transferred over a concept called IP protocol, where each node on a network had an address and the text could be sent to an address.

Later the Transfer Control Protocol was added to the Internet Protocol, designated the TCP/IP network protocol, allowing Packet Switching. Packet Switching is where data is broken into multiple chunks "packets" and sent out with a destination allowing each packet to go through whatever circuit of least resistance to get to the destination. When the last packet arrived at the destination the packets were opened and the text reassembled. This design being totally decentralized allowed for the fastest method of transfer. Shortly thereafter the Simple Mail Transport Protocol; SMTP was added and the first email program was born.

The first high-speed networks were developed and began connecting a third of the country's universities. The increasing number of connected universities and corporations in just one year went from ten thousand in 1988 to one hundred thousand by 1989.

This amazing method of a decentralized communication rejected centralization. The mere critical oversaturation and escalation of cost to contain and facilitate the mounting demand and increased utility caused by the mushrooming amount of additional protocols obstructed every attempt at centralization.

Solutions to time and distance challenges were quickly discovered and implemented. These solutions challenged the time honored methods of previous eras, vanquishing them.

Newspaper, Magazines, Books and Bookstores
The Hyper-Text Transfer Protocol (HTTP) with the corresponding Hyper-Text Markup Language (HTML) quickly replaced printed media, with bookstores and magazine stands losing business to the Internet. News agencies, with their need to have information screened before printing or broadcasting, were replaced with weblogs. This remarkable dissemination of non-central news sources made a "blogger" in Cairo Egypt just as influential as a journalist from the New York Times.

Private and Public Telephones
The Voice over Internet Protocol (VoIP) brought voice from the circuit switching voice network to the packet switching data network. This drastic change made expensive long distance calls cheaper than a simple local call; causing phone companies to scramble to adopt a VoIP solution.

Camera, Film Development, Photos
The Picture Transfer Protocol (PTP) specifies a way of creating, transferring and manipulating objects which are typically photographic images such as a JPEG file. The Media Transfer Protocol (MTP) builds on that allowing inclusion of other file formats. This protocol allows the image to be taken right from the camera and placed into a computer or on the internet for later retrieval, viewing and printing as well as transfer by email or messaged to another individual to view, print

or save to their computer. This protocol removed all centralization and wiped out many photo development companies.

Audio Tape Recording, Vinyl records, VCR, Meetings and Conferences

With the development of audio file format for the internet the music industry suffered great financial losses. The Session Initiation Protocol (SIP) a signaling communications protocol, widely used for controlling multimedia communication sessions such as voice and video calls over Internet Protocol networks lessened the need for being personally present at a distant location.

Personal One on One Visits

The User Datagram Protocol (UDP), computer application sends messages, in this case referred to as datagrams, to other hosts on an Internet Protocol (IP) network without prior communications to set up special transmission channels or data paths which are masterfully utilized with Skype video and audio. This provided an inexpensive alternative to the business quality SIP for the home user.

Movies

Because of the protocol and adaptive programming the movie industry suffered the most. The protocol facilitated home viewers to watch on a big screen any movie past or present on demand. This has forced the movie industry to compete by going to the extreme with enhanced visual and physical experience with IMAX theaters and "state of the art" sound systems and 3D. These are just a few of the examples of "going to the next level" for the movie industry to compete.

Distance has become irrelevant through the power of the internet giving the users instant access to knowledge, books, music, videos, movies in seconds. Contracts and orders for goods and services are done in seconds.

Financial Services, Banks, Check Processing, Currency Exchange, Wire Transfer, Loans

If time makes money then where is the emergence of an internet currency?

If the currency appropriate for a different paradigm of time and distance is misapplied there will be financial disasters and losses.

In our global economy the internet makes state and national borders irrelevant, goods and services are ordered and received within days but payments may take up to weeks to complete through 3rd party mediation.

How would you pay for an internet order from India or China?

Would you ship gold or silver coins?

Would you mail dollar bills?

Would you wire the funds?
This is interesting; in this case the banks on either side of the transaction agree to adjust their books by one bank debiting their ledger and the other crediting theirs; nothing is actually transferred.
The transaction fee the sender pays can depend on the amount being sent, which can be very expensive.

Do you feel safe using your credit card over the internet? Even with seemingly secure sites identity theft is possible. Even large corporations and institutions are not completely immune to cyber break-ins. Credit card info can be stolen and used before the owner is even aware that his personal information had been taken.

Consumers reported paying more than $1.5 billion as a result of credit card fraud in 2011; the median amount consumers paid fraudulently was $537.

http://www.creditcards.com/credit-card-news/credit-card-industry-facts-personal-debt-statistics-1276.php#ixzz2wH2FQNV5

The Original Purpose of a Currency is:
- A common unit of account between two individuals beyond boundaries or borders
- Rare or limited supply
- Maintains value
- Fungible
- Easily broken into equal fractional amounts
- Cannot be inflated or debased
- No third party mediator
- No additional costs
- Transaction time is equivalent to the time transpired in opening of ones purse and extracting the appropriate amount of currency then placing that amount into the hands of another.

Gold, Bank Notes and Credit Cards are for a Previous Era not Now

The internet is by far the fastest method of transacting business until one gets to the payment.

Imagine or maybe you have already experienced, being at your computer seeing and speaking to someone in India or Hong Kong and using collaborating software to go over a contract, discussing each component of the agreement for the goods or services. Then comes the requirement for the first installment of payment or prepayment, what do you do?

What shall both parties agree on for payment? The mailing of gold, silver or Federal Reserve Bank notes for payment is ludicrous. Well there is the "Jet Age" credit card with its additional transactional costs and risk of forgery or ID theft. Or use an international e-commerce business which keeps your credit card information and allows payments and money transfers to be made through the Internet for an additional fee besides the interest charges you receive for using your credit card. If the transaction is between different currencies there will be additional conversion fees. The use of these various business services is subject to the US economic sanction list, and subject to other rules and interventions required by US laws or government.

The problem with having the information of millions of people's credit cards in a centralized location is begging an experienced hacker to "come and get it" and they do! A quick check on the internet with a search engine will convince any naysayer.

Personal financial information should be private!

Imagine you are stopped on the street, pulled aside by a man with a gun and he demanded to know your credit card information and how much money you have in the bank. Wouldn't you think that request a little strange? Would you reconsider answering if it was a police officer? You see, there is something wrong with that request because privacy is our right as American citizens and it is to be protected.

Centralizing this very personal financial information with millions of others is an invitation to disaster.

Returning to our scenario of transacting business over the internet with collaborating software; now, with CPU processors exceeding 4 billion transistors, why can't you initiate an instant transfer of a common unit of account value from your computer to the recipient's?

The First Financial Protocol Over TCP/IP
The Cryptographic Protocol

To understand what it takes to make a cryptographic protocol work for financial services we have to understand the challenges and hurdles that must be overcome.

The first challenge is how to make every transaction private. Well that problem has already been solved through the utilization of advanced military grade layered encryption; Sha256.

The second problem is where the ledger of all the transactions since its inception going to reside and how in a non-centralized network.

The third which has been called the Byzantium Generals Problem is the problem of receiving a trustworthy response in an untrustworthy environment, in other words the network on which you are sending cannot be trusted to respond truthfully.

For my simple mind the challenge and the developed solution is best illustrated as a great symphony where instead of instruments, there are computers which are all performing using their own music at different tempos and it is chaos just like an orchestra warming up.

Now an identical sheet of music is placed before them and the tempo of how they play is determined by the conductor. This metaphor of the sheet music is the ledger of all transactions that have been done previously to the present bar they are now playing. This sheet music or transactional ledger is called, in the cryptographic protocol, a blockchain which is in every participating computer.

The next bar in the sheet music (blockchain) is being assembled as the music is played. To keep the symphony orchestra synchronized the tempo of 6 beats an hour or every ten minutes must be maintained. The conductor is made up of thousands of computers called "miners" that decrypt and calculate. If each processor, that constructs these computers, increases in processing speed they are required to perform greater complex mathematical problems to slow the tempo down, the faster the computers the greater the complexity. If the computers slow down then the calculation complexity decreases to raise the tempo.

The resultant symphony is elegant and precise with the errors of incorrect notes drowned out by the uniform response by the correct notes of the instruments, making that bar permanent as played correctly (establishing a consensus) then written to the sheet music "blockchain" and then they begin the next bar.

Since the metaphor of "playing the music" is actually the transactions or the transfer of ownership of the value of a common unit of account, which in the cryptographic protocol, is either called a token or coin from one computer to another; where do the tokens or coins come from?

The tokens or coins are paid at the completion of each ten minute block to the "conductor" (miners) which are the computers who decrypt and calculate. Then they make the permanent entry for all the transactions in that ten minute timeframe into the ledger "blockchain" in all participating computers as well as set the tempo for the protocol.

What if someone were to modify the blockchain? To modify the blockchain would require greater power then all the computers combined in the cryptographic protocol network whose summation is greater than any super computer now in existence. Additionally, even if there was such a computer and it changed the blockchain, that change would only last until the next beat in the tempo which brings all the computers into consensus occurring every ten minutes, which would remove any change on any of the participating computers.

What about inflation or manipulation of the crypto currencies like what is done to fiat currencies? The standard of the total amount of tokens or coins and when issued is hard coded into the crypto currencies and is not alterable. With Bitcoin a total amount of 21 million will be issued and the times of issuance are preprogrammed with the last one to be issued in 2140.

Are crypto currencies a new epoch? No, the epoch was the concept of decentralization whose proof of concept was the decentralization of the telephone which used the transistor to make the Electronic Switching System.

The Electronic Switching System's prodigy, the internet, with its respective protocols, utilizing the billions of transistors within the CPU's of the computers, have ruptured the controlling walls of containment that centralization enforces.

Now with the first proof of concept for a programmable, encrypted, distributed trust, infrastructure with a neutral transaction currency, Bitcoin, the era of decentralization now turns and moves toward the financial services industry.

"The greatest shortcoming of the human race is our inability to understand the exponential function."
— Albert A. Bartlett

Exponential Growth

In understanding the era we are in and its velocity, that is the rate of change that is affecting mankind and to what depth that change will go; we need to understand the exponential function.

Our minds are designed to think on a linear plane, for instance if we take thirty steps then we would be thirty steps away from where we began. Reality is not constrained by our perception of it. When we take 30 steps exponentially we are a billion steps away from where we began.

In nature there is the exponential growth of bacteria. Bacteria generally reproduce every 20 minutes; which means there is always twice as much bacterium as there were 20 minutes before.

If a mason jar had only one bacterium and given the optimum environment for growth then in 20 minutes there would be two. Then 20 minutes later four bacteria and eight the next 20 minutes and so on. With that knowledge we find the Mason jar is filled at 9:00 a.m. so at what time was it half full? Our brains refuse to think along that path because it is beyond our mental perception. The jar was half full at 8:40, 20 minutes before 9:00 a.m. At what time then was the jar one quarter full? Forty minutes before 9:00 a.m.

Now here is the BIG question. What will be required at 20 minutes AFTER 9:00 a.m.? A whole new jar!

This is why untreated bacterial infections are so deadly. The human body can't respond fast enough to stop it.

Let's look at it another way. Would you work for a penny the first day then 2 cents the second day then continue the doubling each day for thirty one days? With a glimpse of the exponential function the answer would definitely be YES. How much would you earn, not accumulated, but only on the thirty first day? **$10,737,418.24**

On what day did you earn **$5,368,709.12**? You would have earned it on the thirtieth day. Then on what day did you earn **$2,684,354.56**? You would have earned it on the twenty-ninth day.

If you continue this to the thirty-second day you would have earned **$21,474,836.48!**

This is exponential growth.

Now let's examine the Rate of Accelerated Change

4000 B.C.   1800 A.D.   1950   1965   1970

Notice the time intervals between each epoch are decreasing exponentially and the eras are getting shorter.

We are now experiencing a doubling of technological power every two years.

The computers CPU's are doubling in power every 18 months. Additionally the speed, at which they communicate, the internet speed, is doubling in speed every 2 years. At this exponential rate of speed the time of communication and data transfer is cut in half every 2 years!

If any organization or artifact that was designed for the previous eras of centralization is still present today we should be witnessing the walls of its limits beginning to buckle under the stress of the pressure. We should be witnessing areas of the organizations and corresponding artifacts blister and bulge and begin to exhibit failure in their application or function.

This exponential rate of communication expansion MUST be released and given room to expand allowing a new currency and decentralized financial services to grow and coexist or there will be a total systemic failure of all the centralized systems that were designed for previous eras.

Our present centralized financial services that were built and designed for the era of the locomotive cannot survive.

Time makes money. The current financial services industry was not designed to have the ability to respond at these exponential rates of speed, they were built on a response speed of 3 weeks to a month.

Now we have to ask ourselves "Can the internet be stopped?" If it can, then the cryptographic protocol would be stopped as well. If it can't be stopped then neither can the cryptographic protocol of the internet be stopped.

Are the computers and internet going to continue to keep on doubling in power and speed? If the answer is no then the cryptographic protocol will not increase in ability to match the present financial services requirements of this country and ultimately of all nations and become only a technical curiosity. If the answer is yes that they will continue to double then even our wildest imagination for the financial services will not only be met but exceeded.

The following list contains artifacts that are either already decentralized and on the cryptographic protocol, are being developed for decentralization on the protocol or are expected to begin development in the conversion to decentralization and placed in the protocol within the next 2 technological exponential growth cycles, in other words in the next 4 years.

Financial Instruments, Records and Models
Currency
Private equities
Public equities
Bonds
Derivatives (futures, forwards, swaps, options and more complex variations)

Voting rights associated with any of the above
Commodities
Spending records
Trading records
Mortgage / loan records
Servicing records
Crowd-funding
Micro-finance
Micro-charity

Public Records
Land titles
Vehicle registries
Business license
Business incorporation / dissolution records
Business ownership records
Regulatory records
Criminal records
Passports
Birth certificates
Death certificates
Voter IDs
Voting
Health / Safety Inspections
Building permits
Gun permits
Forensic evidence
Court records
Voting records
Non-profit records
Government/non-profit accounting/transparency

Private Records
Contracts
Signatures
Wills
Trusts
Escrows
GPS trails (personal)

Other Semi-Public Records
Degree
Certifications
Learning Outcomes
Grades
HR records (salary, performance reviews,
accomplishment)
Medical records
Accounting records
Business transaction records
Genome data
GPS trails (institutional)
Delivery records
Arbitration

Physical Asset Keys
Home / apartment keys
Vacation home / timeshare keys
Hotel room keys
Car keys
Rental car keys
Leased cars keys
Locker keys
Safety deposit box keys
Package delivery (split key between delivery firm and
receiver)
Betting records

Intangibles (?)
Coupons, Vouchers
Reservations (restaurants, hotels, queues, etc)
Movie tickets
Patents
Copyrights
Trademarks
Software licenses
Videogame licenses
Music/movie/book licenses (DRM)
Domain names
Online identities

Proof of authorship / Proof of prior art

<u>Other</u>
Documentary records (photos, audio, video)
Data records (sports scores, temperature, etc)
Sim Cards
GPS network identity
Gun unlock codes
Weapons unlock codes
Spam control (micro-payments for posting)

Rate of Accelerated Change

On April 15th 1865, while President Abraham Lincoln watched the play in the balcony seat at the Ford theater John Wilkes Booth came in from behind the president and shot him with a percussion cap pistol. Then leaping from the balcony to the stage escaped the theater and rode away on a horse.

On October 3, 1942, Nazi Germany launched a V2 Rocket. It was the first manmade object to break the sound barrier.

Only **75 years**, after Lincoln was shot, which is only one life time; the world saw automobiles, telephones, the Nuclear Bomb, computers, radio, radar, aircraft submarines, and missiles launched into space!

Would a herd riding cowboy or lone Indian scout have recognized the transformation that was in progress when they came upon the first railroad tracks?

Do people today recognize the transformation that is in progress when they use their cell phones and internet?

If we now know the path we are on as well as the velocity at which we are traveling and the resources required to power the travel plus the motivation for the journey; then by examining all previous epochs and eras in comparison we should know where we are and when we will discover the next epoch and enter the next era.

With this understanding of an Age then we should know what we need to do to maximize our efforts within the age we are in and be aware and recognize the coming next epoch.

No Control

Who controls the cryptographic protocol and the tokens or coins on the protocol?
No one controls the protocol, similarly as no one controls the SMTP protocol nor its application email.
Each participating computer is part of the network intelligence which controls the protocol and its application, one of which is the coin or token.

Decentralization is difficult to grasp because our lives are controlled and managed by others. We cannot accept something we have not experienced. The inability to conceptualize decentralization is the result of our own life's experiences because wherever we go or whatever we do is controlled or managed by others.

Centralization is a human social artifact which does not exist in nature, nature is decentralized. The controlling or managing authority is distributed amongst and embedded into the individuals of that species. No one commands the birds to begin their migration or decides the final destination of their migration. The penguins great march across the Antarctic or the golden Plovers migration from Alaska to Hawaii (2300 miles non-stop) is not done by anyone's command or control. No one commands the salmon when to begin their migration up streams and up waterfalls to spawn. The control is decentralized, distributed amongst the members of that species.

Decentralization is resilient and unlimited in potential. As an example let's consider the leaf cutter ants (Atta cephalotes). For over 50 million years the leaf cutter ants have been farming two very important crops that have secured their survival through the greatest devastating global catastrophes which had decimated all the other life forms on earth though leaving the ant untouched.

The leaf cutter ant forages for leaves and brings them to its underground colony where it gives the leaf cuttings to another worker who mulches the cuttings into a paste. Then the paste is delivered to the workers in the garden chamber who then arrange the paste into combs for the growth of fungus that provides the protein and sugars the colony lives off of. The second crop that they farm, are the colonies of over fifty varieties of bacteria that grow on the bodies of the workers in the garden. What makes this second crop so special is that these types of bacteria are the source of our modern day antibiotics. The excretions of the antibiotic bacteria, distributed by the workers from their body as they move about the garden, are spread upon the produce of the fungus thus protecting the food and ants from infections.

Who is in charge of what each ant does? No one is in charge. Who is controlling when and how each ant performs? Each ant is independent and interdependent with no one in control. How do they know to do what they do? The knowledge of what all ants are to do and how is already programmed and hardwired into each ant. Therefore if any one ant is killed another can quickly take his place.

Why are ants so resilient and so difficult to stop or be destroyed? Because there is no centralization, they are decentralized.

What is so revolutionary about the cryptographic protocol?

The protocol enables the creation of applications such as bitcoin to have an unalterable, unforgeable decentralized distributed digital ledger which is the first practical implementation of triple entry bookkeeping. Most important of all is there is no controlling entity.
The protocol is completely decentralized.

Every application built upon this protocol is and will have no centralization, the proof of concept application for the protocol was Bitcoin and now other applications being written will be as well decentralized.

Unstoppable Train

Throughout time revolutionary changes have occurred that have truly advanced mankind to unprecedented levels of sophistication and technical advancement. There are a multitude of proposed justifications for these advances but these I believe are corollary to the motivation that time and prosperity give.
The invention of the wheel and domestication of the horse far exceed in capacity and in less time than what a single or group of men could transport on foot.

Those civilizations who were the first adaptors became the most powerful and prosperous.
We can either close our eyes to the changes or open them wide to the unlimited possibilities.
We can either stand in front of the train to oppose it or climb aboard and ride it.

Welcome the era of decentralization.

Acknowledgments

I wish to express my appreciation to the following:

Andreas M. Antonopoulos
Chief Security Officer at Blockchain.info and Co-Host of *"Lets Talk Bitcoin"* and Author of *Mastering Bitcoin Unlocking digital crypto-currencies,* for his astute, objective and inspirational perspective.

Adam B Levin
Editor and Chief of *"Lets talk Bitcoin"* network
For his provocative, honest and inquisitive investigational reporting on the cryptocurrency ecosystem

A few of the many brilliant minds of developers and coders who guide the future of the cryptocurrency protocol and have lit my imagination:

Jeffrey Paul
Peter Todd
Vitalik Buterin
Charles Hoskinson
Daniel Larimer

Books that have helped prepare me for the era of decentralization:

Simulacra and Simulation (The Body, In Theory: Histories of Cultural Materialism)
by Jean Baudrillard

Science and Sanity: An Introduction to Non-Aristotelian Systems and General Semantics
by Alfred Korzybski

The Third Wave, by Alvin Toffler

Power Shift, by Alvin Toffler

The Republic, by Plato

Last but not least important, is my gratitude to the creator and designer of life in all its complexities, who brought forth all life on earth in less than 3 billion years through his DNA coding and development of decentralization.

www.ingramcontent.com/pod-product-compliance
Lightning Source LLC
Chambersburg PA
CBHW021927170526
45157CB00005B/2218